COELOPHYSIS
and Other Dinosaurs of the South

by Dougal Dixon

illustrated by
Steve Weston and **James Field**

PICTURE WINDOW BOOKS
Minneapolis, Minnesota

Picture Window Books
5115 Excelsior Boulevard
Suite 232
Minneapolis, MN 55416
877-845-8392
www.picturewindowbooks.com

Printed in the United States of America.

Library of Congress Cataloging-in-Publication Data
Dixon, Dougal.
Coelophysis and other dinosaurs of the South /
by Dougal Dixon ; illustrated by Steve Weston &
James Field.
p. cm. — (Dinosaur find)
Includes bibliographical references and index.
ISBN-13: 978-1-4048-2747-9 (hardcover)
ISBN-10: 1-4048-2747-1 (hardcover)
1. Coelophysis—Juvenile literature. 2. Dinosaurs—
South Atlantic States—Juvenile literature. I. Weston,
Steve, ill. II. Field, James, 1959– ill. III. Title. IV. Series:
Dixon, Dougal. Dinosaur find.
QE862.S3D593 2007
567.912—dc22   2006012132

Acknowledgments
This book was produced for Picture Window Books by
Bender Richardson White, U.K.

Illustrations by James Field (cover and pages 4–5, 7,
11, 15, 17) and Steve Weston (pages 9, 13, 19, 21).
Diagrams by Stefan Chabluk.

Photographs copyright Eyewire Inc. pages 6, 18, 20;
iStockphoto pages 8 (Jason Cheever), 12 (Tom
Lewis), 14 (Bill Lucey), 16 (Bruce McQueen); Frank
Lane Photo Agency page 10 (Mark Raycroft).

Consultant: John Stidworthy, Scientific Fellow of
the Zoological Society, London, and former
Lecturer in the Education Department, Natural
History Museum, London.

Reading Adviser: Susan Kesselring, M.A., Literacy
Educator, Rosemount–Apple Valley–Eagan
(Minnesota) School District

Types of dinosaurs

In this book, a red shape at the top of a left-hand page shows the animal was a meat-eater. A green shape shows it was a plant-eater.

Just how big—or small—were they?

Dinosaurs were many different sizes. We have compared their sizes to one of the following:

Chicken
2 feet (60 centimeters) tall
6 pounds (2.7 kilograms)

Adult person
6 feet (1.8 meters) tall
170 pounds (76.5 kg)

Elephant
10 feet (3 m) tall
12,000 pounds
(5,400 kg)

TABLE OF CONTENTS

WHAT'S INSIDE?

Dinosaurs! These dinosaurs lived in what is now southern North America. Find out how they survived millions of years ago and what they have in common with today's animals.

Life in the South

Dinosaurs lived between 230 million and 65 million years ago. The world did not look the same then. In most parts of the world, the land and seas were not in the same places. At times, there were deserts all over southern North America, while at other times, there were rivers and heavily wooded forests.

In the deserts of North America lived armored *Scutellosaurus* and such fierce, meat-eating dinosaurs as *Coelophysis* and *Dilophosaurus*.

5

COELOPHYSIS

Pronunciation:
SEE-lo-FY-sis

Coelophysis was one of the first meat-eating dinosaurs. It traveled around in packs, hunting other animals. Its jaws were long, and its teeth were like steak knives. *Coelophysis* could easily tear the flesh off other dinosaurs.

Hunting animals today

About the same size as *Coelophysis*, the coyote also has long jaws and sharp teeth.

Size Comparison

Life was hard in the deserts of early dinosaur times. Scientists have found fossils of *Coelophysis* gathered around a dry water hole, where the dinosaurs died of thirst.

SEISMOSAURUS

Pronunciation: SIZE-mo-SAW-rus

Seismosaurus lived about halfway through the Age of Dinosaurs. It was the longest dinosaur that ever lived—about the length of three school buses! Its little mouth could not chew food properly, so *Seismosaurus* had to swallow stones to grind up food in its stomach.

Big animals today

The mule deer is one of the biggest animals living in southern North America today. But it is very small in size compared to *Seismosaurus*.

Size Comparison

The name *Seismosaurus* means "earthquake lizard." The ground must have shook as the beast walked.

Alamosaurus was one of the last of the long-necked dinosaurs. It lived at the very end of the Age of Dinosaurs. It ate from the trees that covered the hillsides of southwestern North America.

Tree-eaters today

The white-tailed deer eats from the trees. It has the same diet as *Alamosaurus* did, but it does not eat nearly as much.

Size Comparison

Alamosaurus did not live just in the South. It lived on the hills all over North America at that time.

NOTHRONYCHUS

Pronunciation:
NOTH-ron-EYE-kus

Nothronychus was a strange-looking dinosaur. It had a tiny head and very big claws. It used its claws to rip bark and leaves from the trees. *Nothronychus* was covered in feathers to keep warm.

Tree-destroyers today

The modern beaver brings down trees like *Nothronychus* did, but it uses its teeth to do so instead of claws.

Size Comparison

Nothronychus lived alone in the forests. There was plenty to eat from the trees.

13

DILOPHOSAURUS

Pronunciation:
dye-LO-fuh-SAW-rus

Dilophosaurus was a fast-running, meat-eating dinosaur. It had a very sensitive snout. It ate small animals such as lizards, which it could force out of the cracks in rocks.

Delicate eaters today

The coati has a sensitive snout and delicate paws. It uses these to eat small animals such as insects and lizards, like *Dilophosaurus* did.

Size Comparison

Dilophosaurus had two crests on its head. It used these crests to show off to other dinosaurs.

SCUTELLOSAURUS

Pronunciation:
skoo-TELL-o-SAW-rus

Scutellosaurus was one of the first of the armored dinosaurs. It was only the size of a big lizard. It was covered in little armor studs, which protected it from the bigger meat-eating dinosaurs that lived at the time.

Timid animals today

The chipmunk does not fight with bigger animals. Instead, it hides away from them. *Scutellosaurus* probably did this, too.

Size Comparison

Scutellosaurus was a timid dinosaur covered with more than 300 bony studs. Its name means "lizard with little shields."

ACROCANTHOSAURUS

One of the biggest meat-eating dinosaurs of the South was *Acrocanthosaurus*. It had a low sail down its back that it used for signaling to other dinosaurs. Its long jaws were full of strong, sharp teeth.

Sharp teeth today

The modern alligator has long jaws and sharp teeth, just like *Acrocanthosaurus* did. It is a fierce hunter, too.

Size Comparison

Acrocanthosaurus killed and ate big plant-eating dinosaurs.

DEINONYCHUS

Pronunciation:
dye-NON-i-kus

Deinonychus hunted in packs. It used its claws—including one big, curved claw on one toe of each foot—for ripping into the flesh of other dinosaurs. A pack of *Deinonychus* could bring down the biggest dinosaurs around.

Sharp claws today

The bald eagle has sharp claws on its feet like *Deinonychus* had. But it also has a sharp beak, whereas *Deinonychus* had sharp teeth.

Size Comparison

Packs of *Deinonychus* hunted the many plant-eating dinosaurs that roamed the plains of the South long ago.

WHERE DID THEY GO?

Dinosaurs are extinct, which means that none of them are alive today. Scientists study rocks and fossils to find clues about what happened to dinosaurs.

People have different explanations about what happened. Some people think a huge asteroid hit Earth and caused all sorts of climate changes, which caused the dinosaurs to die. Others think volcanic eruptions caused the climate to change and that killed the dinosaurs. No one knows for sure what happened to all of the dinosaurs.

GLOSSARY

armor—protective covering of plates, horns, spikes, or clubs used for fighting

beak—the hard front part of the mouth of birds and some dinosaurs; also called a bill

claws—tough, usually curved fingernails or toenails

crest—a structure on top of the head, usually used to signal to other animals

desert—a usually hot, dry region with land covered in sand or stones

fossils—the remains of a plant or animal that lived between thousands and millions of years ago

packs—groups of animals that hunt and kill together

plains—large areas of flat land with few large plants

sail—a thin, upright structure on the back of some animals

signaling—making a sign, warning, or hint

snout—the long front part of an animal's head that includes its nose, jaws, and mouth

To Learn More

At the Library

Clark, Neil, and William Lindsay. *1001 Facts About Dinosaurs.* New York: Backpack Books, Dorling Kindersley, 2002.

Gray, Susan H. *Coelophysis.* Chanhassen, Minn.: Child's World, 2004.

Muehlenhardt, Amy Bailey. *Drawing and Learning About Dinosaurs.* Minneapolis: Picture Window Books, 2004.

On the Web

FactHound offers a safe, fun way to find Internet sites related to this book. All of the sites on FactHound have been researched by our staff.

1. Visit *www.facthound.com*
2. Type in this special code for age-appropriate sites: 1404827471
3. Click on the FETCH IT button.

Your trusty FactHound will fetch the best sites for you!

Index

Look for all of the books in the Dinosaur Find series:

MEMORIAL LIBRARY
PO BOX 140
330 BUFFALO ST
SHEB. FLS. WI 53085